SPIRIT OF

LINCOLN

PETER & JANET ROWORTH

First published in Great Britain in 2013

British Library Cataloguing-in-Publication Data
A CIP record for this title is available from the British Library

ISBN 978 0 85710 080 1

PiXZ Books
Halsgrove House, Ryelands Business Park,
Bagley Road, Wellington, Somerset TA21 9PZ
Tel: 01823 653777
Fax: 01823 216796
email: sales@halsgrove.com

An imprint of Halstar Ltd, part of the Halsgrove group of companies
Information on all Halsgrove titles is available at: www.halsgrove.com

Printed and bound in China by Toppan Leefung

Introduction

Lincoln offers a wonderful mix of ancient and modern architecture. The Cathedral is spectacularly placed and it towers over the city and can be seen for up to 25 miles away. This stunning building and the nearby Castle form the core of the 'Uphill' historic area, with its cobbled streets, medieval buildings and specialist shops including boutiques, craft, book and gift shops. Look out for the notorious 'Lincoln Imp', a stone carving in the Cathedral which has become the city emblem. Descend Steep Hill and pass through the Stonebow to enter the 'Downhill' area with its modern pedestrianised shopping facilities. Brayford Pool has been transformed with the establishment of the University and the waterfront has a very cosmopolitan atmosphere with its bars and restaurants. One of the latest developments is 'The Collection', a fantastic new museum combining archaeological finds with fine, decorative and visual arts.

Come and explore the history and heritage, marvel at the achievements of our ancestors in building the magnificent Cathedral, and enjoy all the facilities of a modern, flourishing city.

The Lincoln Imp.

The Millennium Empowerment
sculpture spans the River Witham in
front of the Waterside Centre; its design
was based on turbine blades reflecting
the City's industrial past.

Opposite:
High Bridge, over the River Witham,
is the oldest bridge in England to still
have buildings on it.

Above the central arch of the Stonebow is the
Guildhall which has been in use for centuries as
the meeting place of the City Council.

Opposite: Visitors enjoy spring sunshine as they walk along the High Street.

The Strait starts visitors on the climb to Steep Hill and the upper part of the city.

Opposite:
Jew's House is a superb example of domestic architecture from the twelfth century, while the neighbouring Jew's Court is now the headquarters of the Society for Lincolnshire History and Archaeology.

Visitors descend and climb the
narrow cobbled street of the
aptly-named Steep Hill.

Opposite:
Appropriately called the Readers Rest,
this second-hand bookshop is ideally
situated halfway up Steep Hill.

The Harlequin second-hand bookshop was once an inn of the same name
and stands at the corner of Steep Hill and Michaelgate.

Opposite: The final walk from Steep Hill leads to the open area of Castle Hill.

Now housing Browns restaurant and pie shop, this building provided lodgings for the author T. E. Lawrence (of Arabia) in 1925 whilst he was serving at RAF Cranwell.

Hanging shop signs are an interesting attraction along Steep Hill.

From Castle Hill there is a good view of the Cathedral beyond Exchequer Gate. The Magna Carta public house, on the right, is named after one of the most important documents in English history, a copy of which is on public view inside the Castle.

At the corner of Castle Hill and Bailgate the fine timber-framed building of Leigh-Pemberton House is now the Tourist Information Office.

Newport Arch marks the northern edge of the Roman walled town.
The archway is astride Ermine Street and leads into Bailgate.

Opposite: Lincoln Cathedral towers above
the roofs of Bailgate, as seen from Cobb Hall.

From Lindum Road this narrow pathway and steps leads into Greestone Place and Minster Yard.

Opposite: The fourteenth century gatehouse in Pottergate is now closed off to traffic but it once controlled access to the Cathedral Close.

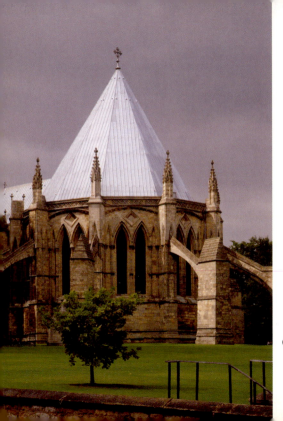

The Chapter House is a decagon with ten sides and it is supported by enormous flying buttresses. It is still used for meetings of the General Chapter, the governing body of Lincoln Cathedral.

Opposite: These attractive houses on Minster Gate form part of the Cathedral Close.

Opposite: Looking up at the west towers of the Cathedral; originally they were topped with spires but these were taken down in 1807 when they were found to be unsafe.

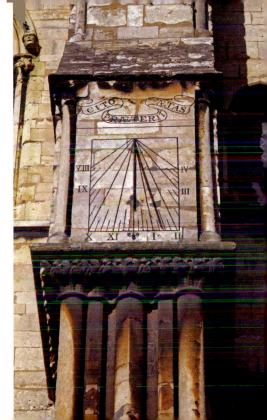

This sundial is high up on the south wall of the Cathedral and would have helped to tell the time in an age when clocks were a rarity.

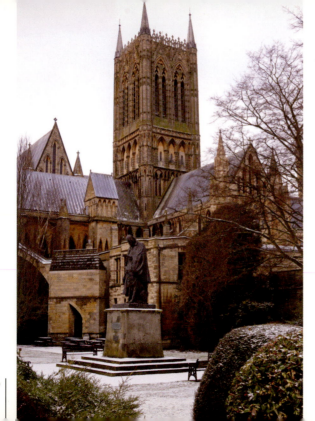

The statue of Alfred, Lord Tennyson was created in 1905 by George Frederick Watts and was placed close to the north side of the Cathedral in Minster Green.

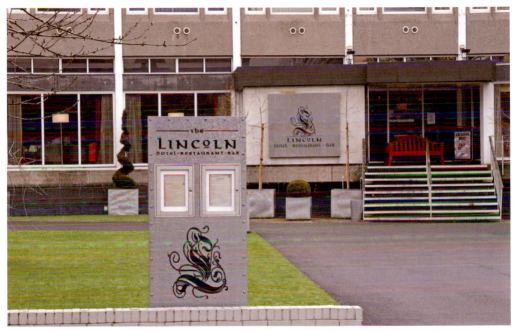

The Lincoln Hotel, designed in the 1960s, has splendid views over Minster Green.

The superb west front of the Cathedral.

Opposite: Take a guided roof tour of the Cathedral and be rewarded with memorable views over Exchequer Gate to Castle Hill and the Castle beyond.

This is the old Gaol set within the Castle walls where prisoners were held during the nineteenth century.

Small gravestones within the Lucy Tower mark the burial places for prisoners who were executed or who died naturally whilst in prison.

The Crown Court building is situated in the grounds of the Castle,
while the water tower beyond has been disguised as a castle keep.

A view from the Castle walls to Ellis's Windmill with the Vale of Trent beyond.

A group of musicians entertain the crowds.

Lincoln shopkeepers are as individual as their shops.

The Collection, opened in 2005, houses displays on the art and archaeology of Lincoln and its county.

The modern architecture of The Collection is in contrast to the nearby
'Uphill' historic area of the Cathedral and Castle.

The Usher Gallery, off Lindum Road, was established in the 1920s to house
the art collection left to Lincoln Corporation by James Ward Usher.

Opposite: This modern sculpture by Michael Sandle entitled 'A Mighty Blow for Freedom'
is set in the Temple Gardens of the Usher Gallery.

A flower seller waits for passing customers near the City Square.

Opposite: Shoppers on Sincil Street.

The attractive glazed roof of Cornhill Market provides shelter for stallholders and shoppers alike.

The Central Library in Free School Lane houses the Tennyson Research Centre; a collection of papers, letters, proofs and the personal library of Alfred, Lord Tennyson.

Majestic London plane trees line the edge of St Swithin's garden churchyard in Saltergate.

Enjoying a rest alongside
Brayford Waterfront.

Opposite: Brayford Pool
is a natural basin at the
junction of the Rivers Witham
and Till, and is linked to the River
Trent by the Fossdyke Canal.
The area was once flanked
by warehouses and busy
wharves but it is now home
to narrow boats and
pleasure craft.

Opposite: Holidaymakers negotiate the low bridge of Wigford Way Flyover as they make their way from Brayford Pool along the River Witham.

During the winter many boats lie moored up at Brayford Pool.

The old timber-framed Green Dragon public house on
Waterside North is dwarfed by adjacent modern buildings.

In Victorian times the landlord of the Adam and Eve public house was forced to remove his new sign when local officials took offence at the naked figures of Adam and Eve!

The main University of Lincoln campus was established
on the southern edge of Brayford Pool.

The modern structure of Sparkhouse Studios and Enterprise@Lincoln contrasts with the University Library which occupies the former sack warehouse belonging to the Great Central Railway.

Opposite: A view over the River Witham towards the Cathedral.

Part of the modern shopping area of St Mark's retail park.

The old St Mark's station yard has now been replaced by modern retail units but the railway theme survives.

Modern superstores can be found on the outskirts of the city.

Opposite: Where once farmers and corn merchants bartered their produce there are now modern shops; the Old Corn Exchange has become Waterstones bookshop while the New Corn Exchange houses a range of retail units.

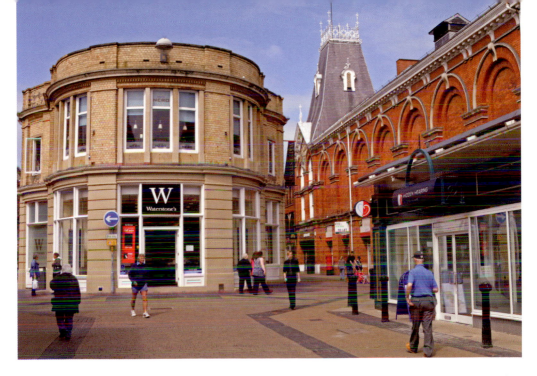

This sign on the wall of the Corn Exchange commemorates 'Snips', the Sealyham terrier, whose owner charged 1d per stroke and raised over £5,000 for charity.

Look out for signs that show where remains of the Roman city
can still be found underneath the present buildings.

The footbridge offers a safe crossing over the
busy dual carriageway on Broadgate.

Opposite: Lincoln is the largest English city to still have traffic
on its main street interrupted by the regular passage of trains.

One of the best views of the Cathedral is obtained from Broadgate footbridge.